Alfred Cridge

Utopia

The History of an Extinct Planet

Alfred Cridge

Utopia
The History of an Extinct Planet

ISBN/EAN: 9783743373433

Manufactured in Europe, USA, Canada, Australia, Japa

Cover: Foto ©Andreas Hilbeck / pixelio.de

Manufactured and distributed by brebook publishing software
(www.brebook.com)

Alfred Cridge

Utopia

UTOPIA;

OR,

THE HISTORY

OF AN

EXTINCT PLANET.

BY

ALFRED DENTON CRIDGE.

PRICE 15 CENTS.

OAKLAND, CALIFORNIA.
WINCHESTER & PEW, BOOK AND JOB PRINTERS,
377 TENTH STREET, NEAR BROADWAY.
1884.

UTOPIA:

OR,

THE HISTORY OF AN EXTINCT PLANET.

PSYCHOMETRICALLY OBTAINED

BY ALFRED DENTON CRIDGE.

CHAPTER I.

Amplitude almost immense,
With stars numerous, and every star perhaps
A world of destined habitation.   MILTON.

I held in my hand a heavy, black stone, not larger than a small orange. It was a meteorite; and as I sat pondering over this strange visitor from starry space, there came before me an old man of mild intelligent countenance, and long gray beard. He was clad in flowing robes of blue and white; and as I gazed on him in wonder he spoke in a strong and melodious voice:

"Son of Earth, would you know the history of the stone your hands clasp?" With eagerness I replied, " Yes, venerable father, it would greatly please me to learn the history of this sidereal visitor, its nature and origin. What was its previous condition in this wonderful universe? What are the laws by which it was cast on the surface of this planet? Tell me that I may learn of the laws of nature, the wonders of the universe, and the wisdom of the Infinite Being!"

Smiling at my eagerness the sage replied;

" My son, law operates through all the realms of the infinite universe, from the drop of water with its microscopic life, or the grain of sand on the dreary desert, to the sun that gives you life or the comet that comes like a dart of the gods through the heavens. The ultimate of all is life, the highest form of which is humanity. The white capped mountain where reigns continual winter has microscopic life in its white fields of resting snow. The dark and crumbling mine has beautiful fungi in its dripping rocks and moldering timbers. Various forms of life are found in the depths of the ocean where man cannot stand, and on the parched desert where he hastens through with death's signatures to mark out his path. The earth, like the tree upon its mountain-side, grows to maturity, ages and dies. So it is with all planets around your parent sun, and with all the infinite number of planets in the extending space of an infinite universe!

" The aim of life on all globes is to produce humanity, the fruit of the tree of life, and when produced, to perfect. True it is that conditions limit or prevent the advent of humanity on many sidereal globes, as conditions prevent the bearing of fruit on many trees that advance toward fruition in a greater or less degree. But life and humanity can exist under many conditions; and as nature has infinite time, humanity will come eventually where now even organic life cannot exist.

" Would you know me by name? I am the genius PSYCHO, and am able to unfold to you many things that the wisdom of your sages has not revealed to your people. Learn and profit by the lessons I will give you, that your earth may grow the faster and the torch of liberty shine the brighter.

" Place the stone you hold in your hands to

your forehead and you will perceive by actual vision a planet in the vigor of youth, the pride of maturity and the disintegration of old age." Doing as the genius requested, in a few minutes, following him, I left the earth behind and then paused to look about me.

The earth was a globe of vapor through which at intervals could be seen portions of continents or oceans as they came into the sunlight. For sometime I remained without moving, to accustom myself to the peculiar circumstances and to observe the wonders of the heavens of which I seemed to be the center, with the stars above and around me. The sun shone with a bright light, yet we were in darkness. As though in a stream of light, but having nothing for the eye to rest upon save the distant stars in the galaxy of the heavens. A signal from Psycho and we went out into space with the speed of light at will. As we went we seemed to go back in time and the heavens changed in appearance. The sun was larger and brighter; the orbits of the planets more extended and in entirely different physical conditions.

After going out until at about the distance of the orbit of Saturn, we came within the influence of a small globe. We circled around it some time and then penetrated its atmosphere. The venerable Psycho informed me that this globe was about two thousand five hundred miles in diameter. I could see that its seas were small, its mountains high and that considerable portions were elevated plateaus.

"This is a world," said the sage, "that had an orbit more oblong than most planets, and being smaller than the earth, passed more rapidly through the various phases of planetary life. It had many natural disadvantages to contend with compared to your world, and but few advantageous conditions above your own. You have the power to go back or forward in time, at will, and thereby to trace the progress of humanity on this globe from its commencement to a civilization that, in spite of many obstacles, far exceeded that reached at present on your earth. But your planet will have a far longer lease of life than had this. Her fiery heart will beat for many ages to come, and your people pass to a stage of civilization as far transcending their present condition as the life of angels does that of cannibals."

As we approached nearer, signs of population in many places could be seen. The cities spread out along valleys or over plains; their houses were large, with wide streets and much open space between. Psycho led me over populous plains, beautiful cities, barren plateaus and rugged mountains, to the vicinity of a small inland town.

We walked along a broad highway, evidently made of artificial stone, toward the town on the farther side of a deep canyon, over which there was a massive stone bridge of a high grade of architecture. On the farther side of the bridge commenced vineyards, orchards and fields of grain.

I noticed that the veins and midribs of the leaves of most of the plants were red, and also that many leaves were red as well. The vines were trained to stout stakes, and standing several feet from the ground before branching out; their leaves were thick and dark green in color. The grapes, red and black, were large and in bunches of many pounds; but I considered the taste inferior to the California muscat. The trees, rarely over ten feet high with dark thick green leaves, bore a delicious fruit which combined the flavor of the peach and plum, and in the pit of which was a sweet oily nut.

But the sun was rising over the dark mountains, and remarking to Psycho that its advent was rather slow, he replied: " Many conditions in your earth are not reproduced here exactly, and, as it would take you some time to discover some of them, I will give you these facts, and others as well, from time to time. The days here are equal to about thirty hours of your time, and are always very nearly of the same length.

" The axis of this planet is nearly perpendicular to the plane of its orbit; therefore the differences in degree of cold or heat, or of the length of day or night, are very slight. The actual year is equal to about thirty-one of your years; but human life is no longer here than it is possible to be on your earth.

" The winter is scarcely perceptible except in elevated lands near the poles, and the summer is only a time of growth. But grains and fruits can be raised at all times; fall, winter, spring and summer, as you understand them in your temperate latitudes, being unknown. The in-

dividual here plants when he likes, and reaps when the crop is matured, the only difference being that in winter the time required for the maturing of grains and fruits is longer than at other times.

"You will now," he continued, "see a people but little in advance in any direction of your own earth. They are where, as far as intelligence and mechanical improvements go, some of your people could be now; but your race will not attain even to this in several generations in all probability."

As the wise Psycho thus instructed my wondering mind, we return to the broad, smooth road, over which a score of our carriages could have been driven abreast with ease. From the town came an individual in a small four-wheeled vehicle drawn by animals; and I observed with great interest this new sight of a brother man in an unknown planet. The animals drawing the carriage strike me at once as peculiar; but little larger than a Shetland pony, they stood like deer, and were about the color of deer when in what is known as "the gray," a grayish blue. Possessing some of the characteristics of a horse, they resembled in some respects the llama of South America. They would be classed in the genus equus by naturalists of earth. They were driven in a span, pulling the carriage by breast-straps, the carriage having a very light tongue between the animals. The carriage is on four low wheels, the front ones being able to turn under the box of the carriage, as do our hacks and trucks. It has but one seat, and in this sits a man who controls his team by voice and a single line. He is a little smaller in stature than the average Caucasian, with large breast, his countenance denoting great intelligence; and except for a slightly yellowish shade of the face, would be taken for a European, though hard to place in any earth race. His face is devoid of beard, but his eyes are large and dark; his hair is long, black and fine. His nose is rather thin, with large nostrils, and his mouth is firm. His forehead is high and massive, projecting well over the eyes. The head covering is a plain cloth cap, and his body is clad in loose garments of a dark color. A light blue cloth, like a blanket or toga, is over his shoulders, and is blown back by the wind, so rapidly do his fleet steeds travel.

We proceed to the town, which is built around a large oval square containing statues, trees and a stone stand in the center for the purpose of open-air meetings. The houses are large, generally of an oval shape with porticos nearly all round, being from about one hundred to four hundred feet long and forty or fifty feet high, having but two stories. The number of houses is not more than twelve or fifteen, and each one has broad grounds with statues, trees, fountains and flowers around it. Some are built of a brown stone, very hard, and Psycho tells me made artificially. Others are white or gray, but each has beautiful representations of vines or flowers on the walls in natural colors.

On the trees in the park I notice some birds resembling mourning doves, but larger; and what strikes me as peculiar is their very long wings and large breasts. I learn this is caused by the rarity of the atmosphere requiring the wings of birds to be longer and more powerful and thus increasing the size of the lungs and breast. Other and smaller birds, some with very brilliant plumage, are flitting around, but their flight is short.

To our right is a round building of gray rock with a dome of brown stone supporting a lower room, also of brown stone. The high portico, with beautifully ornamented pillars and steps that look like burnished agate, make me ask if it is not a temple. "Yes, my son," answered Psycho, "a temple of science. It used to be the temple of the sun, and that female statue to the right of those steps who bears a staff entwined with leaves of the vine was the daughter of the sun and was the female emblem of Nature, Goddess of Peace and Agriculture. On the other side is the son of the sun with uplifted ax; he was God of War, and represents the male emblem of Nature or God. You see they are perfectly nude; for the human form is here looked upon as the highest form of the divine, and therefore not to be concealed. But now this temple is a school and observatory. These and many other statues are no longer adored as representations of the divine, but only admired for their physical representation of the human form. You see the breast of this god would be considered in your world as being too expansive; but here, the air being rare, it is very natural."

We turn to a very beautiful house, with large windows and a magnificent front portico. On each side lie statues of the llama animals, and we wait to see a young man come up the broad path toward us. He is about five and a half feet high, generally resembling the man we saw in the morning. He is dressed in loose yellowish garments, with a purple cloak thrown over his shoulders. A yellow cap, like a smoking cap, is on his head, and his straight black hair reaches down to his shoulders. As he ascends the steps he throws off his cloak, showing a rich, yellowish jacket-like coat that is over a dark garment resembling a shirt, trimmed with silver threads in front. His lower limbs are clothed in a baggy sort of trowsers, also yellow, that are wrapped in the legs of his soft, laced boots or moccasins, the toes of which, for ornament, come to a point and turn over like a skate. As he passes me I find that I am invisible, and that Psycho is also.

The heavy-looking bronze doors roll back as he approaches them, making no noise whatever; and stopping to examine them, I find that they are of a substance resembling paper, and only plated with bronze. An inner set of doors also glide silently into the walls as the soft footsteps of the well-built stranger approach them. But in the apartment of the house I hear a series of soft notes, sounding like a bird's song, that are evidently produced by the opening of the doors. We enter a round hall or parlor, with pale blue walls, on which are beautiful pictures, evidently painted or impressed on the wall itself. In the center plays a fountain into a basin of water surrounding a strong pillar. Plants and flowers are outside of this, and over the floor that is of smooth stone, laid like mosaic-work, are scattered beautiful mats of very rich silken material. Psycho tells me that the silk is a vegetable fiber, and from it, with the hair of the llama-horse and the feathers of birds, is made the soft silken cloak and the yellow garments of our stranger. From a skylight, by means of mirrors, the sunlight is thrown into the room most of the day.

The furniture consists of heavy-looking little tables on castors, but made entirely of paper that is bronzed, silvered, polished or stained as desired. They combine beauty with lightness and are so constructed that by tongues and grooves they can be combined into larger ta-

bles, or even temporary couches. They are very useful, and moving without noise, they are quickly changed at will without confusion. The light chairs with low backs are also constructed of paper, and some of them are on rockers.

On the farther side of the room by the large glass window are seated several persons. Some of them are women, and in dress are not to be distinguished from the men except in ornament and quiet colors. Some are in loose dressing-gowns, but so also are several men; some of the women have very long hair, but here is another with hers rather short. The men are mostly beardless, but one or two have long grey beards and strikingly resemble Psycho in appearance.

The visitor is welcomed by the laying of the hand on his shoulder, he doing the same; and some lay both hands on his shoulder, after which he seats himself on a double chair or settee beside a young girl, and chats with her and others. The language is soft and musical, its cadences striking the ear like music and in some respects resembling the Spanish.

Many people come in from outside and from the apartments adjacent and on the second story. They soon number about one hundred grown persons, with possibly half that number of children over the age of six, the younger ones being left in another room. The several little tables are run together and more from a recess added until two very large ones are formed. On these are placed dishes of fresh, dried and cooked fruits, cooked grain and bread, with milk and syrup. These are brought in on a wheeled dumb-waiter that runs noiselessly in grooves in the floor. It is propelled by electricity and returns the second time before the tables are set. The dishes are light but plated with a substance that resembles glass. They are generally in the form of birds, leaves or fruits, and when dropped will not break.

The people of all ages now sit down to the simple morning meal and merrily chat, often breaking out in song. One child, a little girl of about seven years, of our time, is placed on a little table and sings a very pretty song of her own composition.

All seem happy; and following them through the day I found that out of their day of fifteen

hours long they labored in field or house but five or six. They bathed together in warm baths daily, without regard to sex, and in the afternoon assembled in the park to hear lectures, or in the temple to witness experiments, phenomena, or receive instruction in various sciences. Men and women are on an equality in science, art and litarature, being unrestricted by sex.

Marriage seemed to be with very rare exceptions congenial, and monogamic invariably. Divorce was, in this town of probably three thousand persons, only heard of three or four times in a generation. Often children of the same community married, though generally the parties belonged to separate communities previous to their union. The ceremony was simply an announcement to friends and consisted in registering their names as husband and wife in a public record for that purpose. Motherhood was honorable and parentage was marriage, but seductions were rare and reparation made invariably. The father had to support his children, but to such a point of morality had they arrived that physical enforcement of their laws was only in very rare instances resorted to.

After observing and inquiring for some time Psycho said to me, " Come, my son, and trace the progress of humanity from the brutal cannibal to the intellectual, civilized man. I will reveal to you the steps by which man on this globe eventually attained a civilization higher than this. Come, learn, follow," I obeyed and we turned southward with the speed of the eagle.

CHAPTER II.

The thoughts that he shall think,
Shall not be forms of stars, but stars;
Not pictures pale, but Jove and Mars.

EMERSON.

Soon we came to a broad plain that stretched down to the shores of a long gulf that run up from the ocean much like the Mediterranean sea does from the Atlantic, but only extended about three hundred miles from its strait. The high mountains whose lower portions were covered with timber, ran several spurs into the fertile plains below, dividing them off into valleys. The mountains also fed one large river and several small ones that curved through the sunny valleys to the tideless and seldom stormy gulf. The valleys varied in breadth from the gulf to the main range, being from forty-five to sixty miles and, in some places having a low range of coast hills. The gulf was about twice that width but greatly varied.

We could see that nearly every available spot of land was cultivated and that the houses were large; evidently being communities, like those in the City of the Bridge.

High up on the sides of the foothills and mountains that bounded the fertile valleys were beautiful orchards, vineyards and fields. Here there were finely built cities, but in the hills and mountains they were smaller. The valleys were thickly populated; but the people being in large communities, the farms looked like well-tilled estates of noblemen, only there were no cottages for the laborers. In each valley were one or more places where the communities were closer together, forming villages or cities.

In the largest of the villages nearest the ocean, there bent in from the gulf a bay of considerable size to receive the great river that I afterwards learned was called the River of Snow, from its rising where perpetual fields of snow in the high mountains fed it with coldest and purest water.

Here on the east side of this bay and river, I could see a very large and magnificent city, it being fully ten miles one way by twelve miles the other.

Across the bay was another city that was not so large, and between them ran scores of long narrow boats that moved very rapidly and were propelled by electricity. Between the two cities at one point had been built a bridge of highly ornamented stone, that was at least five miles

long. Over it ran carriages, drawn by the llama-horses or propelled by electricity. Broad highways of smooth stone extended from these cities in many directions, and out in the gulf were many ships coming and going.

I remarked to Psycho, "What a large city this must be. It is as large as London; let us go down in it; I should like to see the people who appear so highly civilized."

"The two cities together are about as large as London; but do not contain so many inhabitants," replied Psycho, who continued:

"These cities together do not have half a million inhabitants, as no houses except public buildings are allowed to be over two stories in hight. Here each building must have around it four times the space it occupies, besides the wide streets and avenues. In addition to this one block in sixteen is devoted to public gardens, parks or assembling squares for the people. Restrain your eagerness to observe these people; I have much yet, my son, to show you before you go among them."

We went up the gulf to where a river ran through a valley where the gulf had extended; and here was a city of about four miles square, and the valley was as thickly inhabited as well as cultivated as those along the gulf.

On the south side of the gulf were low hills not very thickly inhabited, containing but few communities. This I learned was because of the poorness of the soil and the scarcity of water.

On still further we came in sight of a large and clear lake that was ninety miles long and from thirty to forty wide, with several beautiful islands set like gems both in cluster and solitaire in its western portion.

There also was a beautiful city here where the lake was drained by a short river running into the gulf. A canal connected it with the ocean, and around the lake was a rich, populous and fertile land. We did not stop, however, but continued to pass over several countries all highly civilized, Psycho giving me considerable information about them as we went.

Again we were over the City of the Gulf, and Psycho spoke to my eager ears: "You have seen, son of Earth, that this globe is inhabited by a race of human beings that are highly civilized, intelligent and progressive. Want, fam-

ine and war are now unknown; and soon you will go among them and observe their superior civilization. But first it will be best for you to commence at the beginning of humanity on this planet, and trace its progress from age to age."

The curtain of time rose as he ceased to speak. Back into the ages with faster and faster speed turned the globe.

Before us at the will of Psycho, the gulf grew wider and larger, and the ocean overspread the plains, while the plateaus became covered with verdure. The mountains sank and the globe grew hotter with the heat of the internal fires. Tropical vegetation overspread the plains and valleys; and first but a few and then none at all of the mountains reared their heads in helmets of snow.

All signs of civilization had disappeared.

Now we descended to one of the semitropical continents and wandered through the dense forests of that primeval time. Birds larger than the ostrich stalked by the muddy river, fishing for the large green frogs that were in the slimy pools of stagnant, black water. Turtles lurked in the sun or slowly proceeded to their nests in the hot sand-banks. Gay colored birds screamed in the branches of the trees, or industriously gathered insects in the air or on the moldering logs. Great serpents lay coiled in the branches, and with glittering eyes waited for the wary monkey or hunted the eggs of the indignant and loudly protesting birds.

Great proboscidians crashed through the forests, bathed in the shady pools or lay in the long grass of the glades. Here in the jungle crouched the fierce tiger or the surly lion. From his cave in the hill-side shuffled the mammoth bear on his way to the banks of the river to slake his thirst. The fierce-eyed wolf stalked to his den above the gliding waters, and near him crouched the fox, intent, sly, and watchful. And down the stream floated great saurians like lifeless logs.

But here in the æons of the past was MAN, rude, naked, and hairy. In his arms a rudely sharpened stone or a heavy club. Of large frame, muscular; his forehead low and covered with masses of dirty, unkempt hair; a protruding jaw and skin of brown,—truly he looks hardly human.

He lives in caves with his tribe of perhaps a score besides himself. His food is the wild fruit and berries, the putrid flesh of animals, the eggs of birds, the fish that swarmed in the river, or anything alive or dead capable of supporting life.

If belated, a hollow tree or its spreading branches will serve him for a resting place and his stout club will protect him from any wandering foe that may desire to make a meal of him. When with his sturdy brother-cavemen and hunger urged them on, they would attack even the mammoth cave-bear and overpower him with swiftly hurled stones and swinging blows of clubs. Or they would lure the elephant by enraging him with dropping or throwing stones to chase them into the marshes, where they would finish him.

At one period a mountain arose out of the plain and belched forth streams of lava that, flowing into the river, turned its course. Fire was before them. But they did not realize the value of the gift; and, though greatly wondering at the phenomena, they made no effort to preserve the red, biting rock, and after a time it died out. At another time lightning shivered a tall tree, and set the dry leaves on fire around it, as two hunters were hastening to the tribal cave. They stopped to examine the peculiar creature from the skies; for so they regarded it, and eagerly watched it lick up the leaves and splinters. One seeing its fondness for leaves, piled some on the flames; and they laughed with child-like glee when the bright blaze reached up and lit the gathering darkness. But when they had gathered all the leaves in the immediate vicinity and the strange animal had bitten their fingers and toes several times, they left it to die out.

The patriarch of the tribe who was bent with age and whose head was gray with the marks of time, was eagerly told of this peculiar adventure and asked for its explanation. He remembered that when a boy a tall tree in the river bed surrounded by a pile of drift-wood had burst into flame that burned long after the shower that was descending; and so he gave to his auditors the wisdom of his fathers and some of his own opinions. This, he explained, was a sign of anger from the Sun-god at being shut out from the sight of earth, his wife, by the clouds; and so with shouts of thunder and fierce blows of lightning-clubs, he forced his way down in spite of them. He told them of a youth who many years before had refused to give a portion of his game to the old men warriors, and while leaning against a tree was struck dead by the incensed Sun-god that roared in a voice of thunder: " Die, ungrateful and undutiful son!" and the wondering savages doubted not.

But at last fire came as a gift to stay; and then commenced the upward progress of humanity. The aged with fire made better weapons, and the warriors were enabled to kill the savage beasts around them and frighten off others. Agriculture was discovered; at first it was but a few seeds thrust into the ground with the finger. Then a rude stick and next a flint hoe were used to plant the scanty crops, which, when harvested, enabled them to keep starvation away from their caves in time of want; and thus cannibalism as a necessity was at an end.

In this world copper was very scarce, and so the people had made considerable progress with stone implements and weapons before they discovered a soft, whitish, very light metal to work with. They soon found iron, of which mountain ranges were almost entirely formed in some places; and then they pushed on faster still.

The inquisitiveness of man that led him to question and to theorize, founded religion.

The youths asked of the old men of the tribe explanations of the things they could not with satisfaction account for; and the fathers of the tribe answered to the best of their ability and information, often making up theories on the spur of the moment to conceal their ignorance from the young. These theories became by age divine dogmas that it was dangerous to controvert; and thus religions were established. As tribes grew into nations it became necessary to specially instruct certain youths in the legends of the fathers and the traditions of their people; and in this way priesthood was established. The great and victorious chief of a hundred battles was at death sorrowed over; and by the hut fire or around the council of war, his great deeds, gradually growing in size and valor, were recounted by his people, his small deeds being forgotten. As time went on and tribes became

nations a score of names were mingled with his and his deeds; and thus exaggerated were put in the life of one man; and then the next step was to deify such a prodigy. He was declared to be the son of the Sun-god and the God of man. Priests claimed to bow before him and hold conversation with this mighty being. Thus they obtained the direction of the nation and made themselves all-powerful in its councils.

With the advent of man came war; and for ages with torch and sword races fought with races, nations with nations, tribes with tribes; and the labor of years, the civilization of centuries, were washed away in streams of human blood. Whole continents were overwhelmed by invading armies who, after seizing on the country, held it until in turn conquered by others of their own or of some different race. In various places the light of civilization rose high; but being built in nearly every case, on slavery, blood, war and injustice, it fell but to burn the brighter elsewhere in the centuries that succeeded. Or Wrong seized upon the temple of Progress and built within a throne guarded by Superstition and Ignorance; and though Science was chained by tyranny and injustice, she still lived to finally rule supreme.

Just as it looked as if a people were ready to take wings to their feet and fly ahead, they would be overrun by lower nations; or a revolution caused by human slavery would reduce them to semi-barbarism. Fierce wars on customs and religions were waged by the most progressive nations, the priests and aristocratic rulers encouraging them. For by keeping the people in ignorance and fighting some one else, they kept control of the state. Two races fought for a long time on the question of whether the sun was a god or not; and if he was, did he have two children, male and female, without a mother? The one claimed that the sun was a god and the father of the male and female in the universe; the others held that the sun was his own creator and that the goddess of the female or spiritual was co-equal and co-existent with the god of the male or material.

On these questions the two races in various nations fought at intervals for centuries, and when resting fought with themselves to keep up the art of war.

But at last the idea of LIBERTY began faintly and vaguely to illuminate the minds of advanced thinkers. One isolated people, few in numbers, early obtained for themselves a liberal form of government that we should call republican; and they retained it with slight modifications century after century, rarely disturbed by foreign wars or internal dissensions. In the land by this gulf, which they called what would mean the Gulf of the East, the people called themselves free, and changed the name of the country from its ancient name to one that meant Liberia. Yet they held slaves of a race of dark, fierce mountain people that lived on the plateaus to the north; also of a light-skinned people like themselves, and of a brutish, savage race that originally came from a continent to the southeast. While they cheered for liberty, the haughty rich drove slaves in chariots and lashed them like dogs. A man could sell his children or himself into perpetual slavery; and yet they were free, according to the statements of their orators and tyrants!

And they had made progress in mechanics and arts meanwhile. Populous cities, well-cultivated fields, costly palaces, grand temples, magnificent public buildings, immense and well equipped standing armies were to be found in several countries.

The people to the south of Liberia were about equal in civilization with the Liberians and though differing in religion, customs and manners, they were very progressive. These people were tall, slightly brown, very brave, with pink eyes and very black hair. The two races ultimately commingled so as to be alike in nearly every respect. But beside their boasted civilization and liberty dwelt barbarism and slavery. The well-tilled fields were worked by the weary slave beneath the driver's lash. The populous cities were filled with toiling free slaves and bond slaves. The temples and palaces were next door to straw and mud huts; and the mansion of the land-owner was in sight of the hovels of the land-worker. Toil and slavery, luxury and ease, privation and waste, made startling and significant contrasts.

While the rich reveled in costly dinners and rioted in extravagance otherwise the poor lived on a few roots and boiled grains or starved by thousands in their cheerless hovels. The massive temples and statues were reared by toiling

slaves who lived in rude shelters of sticks and mud around them. Ignorance among the slaves and lower classes was encouraged; vice, disease and famine came in to keep it company.

To the north of Liberia, the dark Arab mountain people lived in tents or rude walled cities, and often attacked the people of the plains. But the Liberians were brave and more skilled in the manufacture of armor of steel, and so were enabled to make slaves of the mountaineers; very often they returning the favor. When at peace they traded various trinkets, armor, cloth, etc., for skins, llama horses, small black cattle, and the precious copper of the plateaus. The Arabs worshiped idols, evil spirits and the spirits of their ancestors, and often made human sacrifices.

They several times poured down into the gulf plains and held possession when the Liberians were weakened with fighting the people of the lake country or with themselves. But in a few generations they would become Liberians and fiercely fight the Ar..bs from whom they were descended.

Alcoholic wines and liquors were early manufactured; but they had also a peculiar root that was something like opium and tobacco in its effects when chewed. It was somewhat bitter, but was ground up and mixed with sugar and gum. A little of it was a stimulant; but when several bites were taken it produced a sort of quiet semi-conscious stupor that enabled the user to forget he was hungry and to be utterly regardless of the future. Its use was encouraged amongst the slaves and the poor by the rich, and steps to have it expelled from the country were for a long time unsuccessful.

The priests had great control over the masses, and were desirous of keeping them in ignorance; for the interest of the aristocrats and the priesthood were the same. They therefore preached into the drowsy ears of the disturbed slaves the sanctity of government and the wickedness of revolution.

The aristocrats bought and sold slaves, as they did their horses, goats or little black cattle.

The free poor looked with contempt on the wretched slave; and by discreet management the discontent of one was used by the masters to hold in check the discontent of the other.

Temples were reared and retinues of priests kept them in ignorance. These cities were crowded and unhealthy. The greed of these men was such that air, room, and sunlight were denied to the poor, only those who could pay well for them enjoying what rightly belonged to all. Pestilence and famine swept the rich and poor, but yet the aristocrats kept their grip. The cry of Liberty was heard from the slaves. The priests counseled moderation, joined in their councils, and when they could no longer persuade them to pray and petition their masters, betrayed them.

The slaves arose but were slaughtered by thousands and their bodies piled up and burned. And the free poor did the killing for the rich who commanded them. Again and again they arose, each time betrayed and cursed by the aristocratic priests and each time had to fight the free poor, who only got their labor for subduing the slaves. But eventually chattel slavery was abolished. The slaves were free, but the free were slaves; they soon found they had exchanged the lash for starvation; and the whole people revolted, burning, killing and destroying, only to again change the form of government and to put aristocrats on top in less than a generation. The rude Arabs united together and threatened to destroy the nation, when a discovery was made that revolutionized the art of war. That was a bomb that was fearfully destructive. It was thrown from a small light cannon and exploded in from five or six seconds to half a minute as desired after leaving the gun.

The inventor's name corresponded as near as I can transcribe it to. Loay. He was a refugee Liberian in the country of the Lake people, having fled from his own land after assisting in an unsuccessful attempt at revolution. A chemist and a machinist by profession he got the idea of bombs, and thought by secretly perfecting them, his brother revolutionists all over that world in various nations would be enabled to overthrow tyranny and crown Liberty.

The country around this large lake was called by a name equivalent to SUNLAND, because of its people being sun-worshipers; and hereafter I shall so designate it instead of the Lake country.

Upon his arrival at Lake city, Sunland, he

went among his fellow revolutionists who were natives of Sunland and also those who were exiles, like himself, from Liberia.

Loay was highly connected in Liberia, his father having been a man of wealth and rank; and the son of his oldest brother was then a general in the royal army of Liberia.

In Lake city Loay met with a Sunlander who was a mechanic or metal-smith whose name sounded similarly to Coruala, and to him he confided his plan; Coruala was quickly fired with the ideas and patriotism of his middle-aged confider, and went into it with all the ardor of youth. Coruala and Loay put each the little money they had into the purchase of chemicals, metals, etc., for experimenting and for the rental of a cellar in a quiet portion of the city. Coruala had a friend, a chemist and a potter, Mardola; and upon his being told of their project volunteered to put in the little hoard he had saved, and to assist as he could with his earnings as potter or chemist. They toiled and worked for several of our years to get their bombs perfected.

At last they got them so that the chemicals were put with pieces of iron, spear heads, etc., into a hollow clay globe which Mardola had invented, and this was put into a rude cannon the invention of Coruala and would explode upon violently striking any object.

Coruala and Loay next invented a sort of electric fuse that would explode the bomb in about five seconds from its time of expulsion from the cannon and made the bomb of paper and clay so that it was not so fragile. Also, it would not explode by concussion as the earlier ones did.

Having reached this point Loay began to make arrangements to teach his fellow revolutionists in Liberia, as well as Sunland, how to make them and sent several over to Liberia that were used to shake up the residence of the king a little. But Coruala had, while toiling in the dark, damp cellar, with straw for a bed and a little grain and fruit for food, fallen in love with a young mechanic's daughter and was engaged to her.

He desired to starve and toil no more, and so informed his partners Loay and Mardola. They were indignant and only desired to make a bare and scanty living that the revolutionists might overthrow the aristocrats. Coruala wanted to dress his wife in golden cloth and ride in a chariot, live in a fine house and "fare sumptuously every day." His partners refusing to accede to his demands to charge for their bombs and retain the secret, Coruala privately went to the official, who would here be called the Secretary of War, of Sunland, and had an audience with him. War was about to be declared between Liberia and Sunland, as the Sunland government had found that the Arabs were preparing to make war on the Liberians. Thinking to force the Liberians by attacking them at this time to compel them to give up a group of valuable islands they possessed in the only ocean, the Sunland government were massing troops and building iron war-ships with all haste.

The minister listened to Coruala with attention, and requested him to call again the next day, giving him several pieces of copper money which were nearly as precious as gold is to us.

Upon returning to the cellar he had an armful of provisions, and thus aroused the suspicions of Mardola. When in the morning he hid three hand bombs in a basket and started for the residence of the Secretary of War, Mardola followed at a safe distance, and then seeing him enter started back to warn Loay. But Loay had gone to a secret meeting of the revolutionists to introduce his bombs and did not return for several days. Coruala went with the minister away from the city and showed the force of his bombs by setting them off against some large rocks, and told how he thought a cannon could be improved so as to cast the bombs possibly half a mile, but he lacked money. On his return he was given a large fortune for the receipt, and his ideas and his ambition were thus satisfied. He hastened to find Mardola, but that discreet individual had fled, leaving all the bombs, which Coruala now moved to the royal armory.

Coruala wrote a letter to his partner Loay inviting him and Mardola to come and share his good fortune, but Loay replied with such bitter reproaches that the government was induced to put a price upon his head. On hearing of this Mardola hastened to Liberia and there sold the secret to the Liberian government for a large sum of money and a grant of land.

He wrote to Loay and Coruala saying he had decided to blow himself up, as he no longer desired to live. Loay dodged about for some time but at last without money or friends made a secret visit to Coruala, and at the point of the knife got money to leave the country. He would have killed him but for the pleadings of his young wife. From Sunland he went to a little republic across the ocean and there died after seeing his invention annihilate one race and enslave his countrymen.

The Liberians rejoiced and marched against their enemies, completely subduing them in a few months and seizing on their country.

Fortunes were made from the copper mines, and other natural resources of the conquered country; but the masses were in poverty and degradation as before.

After cherishing what remained of their liberty for sometime, they arose by thousands against the growing despotism of the higher classes. But the bomb guns, now highly improved, destroyed them wherever they assembled. Terrible was the loss of human life; and the people found it impossible to effect anything in securing their rights by massing in large numbers. They subsided into sullen, hopeless slavery for a few years; but then they utilized the lessons they had received, and proceeded to effect their liberty by the very means their masters had used to conquer them. International war and rebellion was at an end, but revolution was not; and the aristocrats were powerless with their armies or their guards.

The revolutionists, after being again and again subjected by fearful slaughter, at last commenced to use bombs themselves. The tide turned and aristocracy once more began to tremble. But by strict watch, money and power, the government managed to destroy the plans of the revolutionists, buy their leaders, and execute those who in attempting to carry out a plan were caught. It was a crime for citizens to have, sell, buy or make cannon bombs, or even have in possession the materials to make bombs. They were manufactured by the government only, with great care, and any one caught with bombs, cannon, manufacturing, buying or selling them, was put to torture and killed. Screws of steel were thrust into the flesh, heated red hot by electricity, and twisted and thrust into the gagged victim until he told of accomplices, confessed or died. If publicly executed a shock of electricity killed him and his body was burned. In Liberia the body was especially preserved, as it was a part of their religion to keep the body whole. But the revolutionists soon got over the error arising from this religious belief.

The masses were educated in certain respects, but only in those ruts that the aristocrats and priesthood desired. Not only was religion taught, but also superstition; and when science came against the dogmas of the priests, it was suppressed in the various schools and colleges of the state and the educational institutions of the aristocrats.

Political and social dogmas were taught as self-evident and not to be questioned that had no foundation whatever in fact, but helped to keep in mental bondage the many students of the lower orders. Those who were able to perceive the fallacy of these theories and doctrines were held in contempt by the all-wise teachers.

Inventions of great utility were being rapidly developed, and art and science were making great progress; but the people found themselves very little better off, while the aristocrats increased in power and wealth. The mechanical and mental improvements had outstripped the political and moral. Regardless of the will of the people, whose servants they professed to be, the aristocratic politicians outraged all sense of honor or trust, and grew rich from the taxes levied on the people.

CHAPTER III.

"She saw her sires with purple death expire,
Her sacred domes involved in rolling fire,
A dreadful series of intestine wars."   POPE.

The invention of the bomb and cannon and the subjection of their enemies of the hills, together with the utter abandonment of war with their sister nations, only made the masses feel the lash more keenly. Numbers and money were supreme, and with standing armies collected from among the people, well-filled treasuries from the same source, and the merciless and repeated use of bomb-cannon at every effort of the people to assert their rights, the aristocratic classes were without fear of the masses.

But the revolutionists were not quiet long. From their martyrs who had fallen before the bombs of their fellow-slaves, the soldiery, they learned and remembered lessons.

A meeting of revolutionists in Liberia was held one night in a low cellar for the last time before making a long-planned attack on the aristocrats during a grand procession to be held the next day. Suddenly a force of gens-d'armes broke in upon them and seized every one they could lay their hands on. Their earnest workers, as they fled, carried one of the cannon and several of the bombs with them a little way, but being hard-pushed concealed them in a large paper box in a back yard. (They made boxes of stiffened paper, serving the same use as wooden boxes do with us.) In a few nights they returned and conveyed it by several stages to a little mountain farm quite a distance from the city, and buried it. There they patiently worked, planted a crop, and manufactured bombs. One worked as a potter, and then, after much scheming, got a job in the government bomb factory; but he was so inquisitive that they discharged him and kept a strict watch over his movements. But he carefully kept away from his friends and toiled in a pottery to keep them in funds.

At this time there were from forty to fifty unitary communities in the country, where from a score to perhaps a hundred families lived under one roof, and co-operated in business matters as farmers or manufacturers. Many, from inability of individuals to agree or from the laws that interfered with their action, had given up. Since the restoration of the arbitrary government of the aristocrats communities had been discouraged, because of the revolutionary tendencies of many of their members. In the valley below the little farm of our three plotters was one of the largest and most progressive communities in Liberia, many of the members being revolutionists. Here the two who remained on the farm obtained work whenever they desired it, but refused to join their friends as they were working for a certain object, and to join them would be to give it up.

After about three years of our time another grand religious and military procession was decided upon and announced, and the three revolutionists resolved to be there. A rude wagon was filled with some rather poor dried fruit they had bought for speculative purposes, expecting to make a corner in it. Under this they had their cannon, and in front they had a lot of large bombs and a box of hand-bombs, all well covered with dried fruit. To this wagon they hitched six horses, as I shall hereafter call these peculiar animals, and ill clad the two farmers started for the capital of Liberia, overtaking on the road the potter, who was disguised as a very old woman.

On the morning of the great holiday and procession our friends are located on the main avenue, vending their fruit to the waiting crowd. The gens-d'armes come along and rudely order the ignorant peddlers to leave the street, for his majesty, the father of the people and the representative of the sun, is to make his appear-

12

soon with his nobles, priests and army, on his way to the great temple to offer prayers for the nation.

With great trepidation they hurry into an adjoining alley and awkwardly leave their wagon across the pavement only to be ordered on by another party of gens-d'armes and roundly abused for their stupidity and ignorance. The elder farmer scratches his teeth (the customary sign of satisfaction among those people) and smiles to his companions. Slips of paper with the order of the procession, are distributed by boys, and flowers are strewn in the street by a large number of girls and maidens. These slips gave the plotters exactly the information they wanted.

The head of the procession appears, and the plotter proceeds to cover up the fruit with a cloth. Next he unearths the cannon, getting it ready for work under the cloth, and his companions wait at the back of the wagon with folded arms. With pomp and display the army, with clanging bands and glittering banners, passes by; but the peddlers do not make a move. Priests in robes of white, with urns of burning incense, pass, followed by carriages with proud aristocrats. Still they wait.

Now in glittering armor, with silver stars on their helmets, march by a superb body of men; these are the royal guard and are the picked soldiers of the army. Then precede and follow the king, his nobles and high priests. Here comes the large blue and yellow banner of his majesty, and now the peddlers lay their hands on the concealing cloth ready to lift it at the right instant.

Nearer, nearer on a palanquin borne on the shoulders of men and surrounded by a trusty guard and the chariots of his nobles comes the ruler of the people. The potter in the wagon says " Now !" The cloth is torn aside and at a touch of the potter's foot a bomb is cast into the proud nobles. But though his palanquin is dropped, the king is unhurt. " Quick, another!" cries the potter, and a second bomb is cast into the procession, tearing the haughty, fleeing king into a hundred pieces. The citizens fly for their lives; the royal guard rally round the spot where their masters are slain. They, the sons of noblemen, are torn to atoms by the revengeful and destructive bombs. The remaining guards endeavor to flee; but their companions push them on to destruction. The three revolutionists are now out of cannon bombs, and the desperate guards make a dash for them; but hand-bombs hurl them back. The cannon and fruit are dumped out of the wagon as the horses are furiously driven into the next avenue by the potter and his companions. A body of gens-d'armes endeavor to interrupt their flight, but are driven off by a volley of hand-bombs. Another body only wait to see two of their number fall, to run.

Now the soldiery with bomb cannon chase the fugitives in hot haste, but so many of them jump on the flying chariots that the panting horses cannot overtake them. See ! an electric carriage flies by with express speed, but the ground gets rougher as they leave the city, and the fugitives still keep on.

Through all this uproar not the bark of a dog is to be heard. There were no dogs on this globe, the last of the small wolves having been killed generations ago. But the very large cats might have been seen running in all directions. The fugitives turn suddenly aside into a piece of woods by the river side, leave their team, change their garb and separate, shortly joining the eager crowd of soldiery, police and citizens who were chasing them, and inquiring what all the commotion meant. The city is given up to wild mobs, for the soldiery are demoralized.

The crowded, filthy portions of the city are set on fire, and the water-pipes cut by a band of men who have been fighting the outrageous rack-rents that their landlords have forced them to pay for the miserable death-traps. Advantage is taken by the mob during the panic to sack the houses of the rich and rob the temples of many valuables.

But on the morrow order is restored by the army, and a new ruler takes the royal staff in his hand and wears the glittering diamond seen on his head-dress. The aristocrats have learned a lesson and the revolutionists take new courage. After the new government had put to torture and executed several scores of victims, it proceeded to make some concessions of a trifling character to the people.

A party of revolutionists soon began to secretly store explosives in the cellar of the national

representative chamber. But as several of them had friends in that body and had warned them to stay away, the plan fell through, as only a part of the explosive went off shaking the building and killing but a few.

Four conspirators then began from their hovel to tunnel under a nobleman's residence that was a long block away from them. This nobleman gave parties or balls attended by the great dignitaries of the state and church.

The four worked patiently for months, first to dig the tunnel, then to obtain and place the explosives deep under the beautiful residence of this nobleman. No one knew of their project and no warning was given; but one night when revelry was at its hight in the beautiful palace, the four toilers met in the hovel and the electric flash was sent along to start the horrible work of destruction. The whole city was shaken as if by an earthquake; for the revolutionists put in more than enough to do the work. Great rocks crushed through the roofs of houses all around; bodies of the fair, the brave, the innocent, and the guilty were blown high in air or torn into atoms. One rock crushed through the hovel of the breathless conspirators, instantly killing one, and severely wounding another. Fearful of being betrayed his comrades killed him, and separating, fled.

The revolutionists, now greatly encouraged, formed into bands of three and four, and prepared to enforce their rights. First they threatened and got nothing, then they placed harmless bombs in public places and observed their effect on the people. Sometimes a bomb was found that would go off, and several of these proved very destructive. Next they proceeded to revolt but were quickly quelled, the ignorant mob foolishly rushing to the public buildings, to be scattered by bombs. A strong fierce leader was found by the aristocrats and was declared "defender of the gods," etc., and after ruling with merciless severity, and having apparently destroyed the revolutionists, he made a grand march driven in a costly chariot with guards and artillery and other soldiers numbering thousands before and behind him. When he reached a certain square we see parties of three or four together come around the fruit-stand from the sewers and other places of concealment underground.

See! they have bags of bombs and drag cannon out of cellars from under fruit stands and even tear them up from under the pavement. The gens d'armes make a dash for them, but are routed by the desperate revolutionists who expected them. All the revolutionists are now massed and up and down the broad avenue; quickly, skillfully and effectively they pour in the destructive bombs regardless of their own individual safety. The "defender" and his nobles are destroyed, and his army driven with great slaughter into the grand royal gardens. Here they endeavor to use their artillery on the revolutionists, but with little effect, for they never find more than half a dozen together and if they attempt to seize them are blown up by the reckless revolutionists. The mob knows better than to assemble and the revolutionists are victorious.

One man of a trio touches the electric spring of a bomb, when his comrades are suddenly seized and standing over it fight as if for life until it explodes and tears a score of men into shreds, including the operators.

The demoralized royal army raises an artificial white bird (a sign of truce) on a pole and beg to be allowed to surrender to some one.

But after obtaining such a victory and organizing a constitutional government the revolutionists divide off into factions and in a few years the aristocrats are again in power. They get a dictator and a sort of senate and proceed to run in the old way. The revolutionists again conspire, and this time with rapidity. The dictator is seated with his senate in the great temple of liberty when a man walks up to him and humbly asks that a petition be granted, and is put off with evasive answers. He begs instant action but is constantly put off.

He turns to the senate and then to the dictator surrounded by his guards and says in effect: "Traitors, your time has come. So die all enemies of humanity!" His foot touches a secret spring under the rich carpet; he stamps on it; the senate spring to their feet, but as they do so a terrific explosion takes place, and not a man escapes.

After various attempts of men to assume royal powers under various names and they, and their armies are destroyed, power is not desired. To appear with a guard meant death, and to

betray the trust of the people was equivalent to suicide. Justice was linked with liberty and the people were made the final appeal of the nation. More than once men of the purest motives were destroyed by their enemies; but the revolutionists generally were careful before condemning a man in power, to give him a chance to resign or reform.

Eventually, after having several forms of a democracy, a constitution was formed scarcely containing a thousand words, and woman was given full power with her brothers. Then the country started after the long period of riot, discord and revolution, on an era of peace. The ownership of land was abolished, no house in any city or district could be over two stories high, and the cities were given room.

The function of government was to construct public works, represent the people in all national matters, issue money and protect its citizens. Each city, district and community managed its own affairs, and in any public question pertaining to a district its people decided it; if to the nation the whole people decided it. Laws were few and brief. Thus, lawyers, beggars and millionaires were not to be seen. Labor was honorable, idleness a disgrace. But toil was banished and slavery under any name, at an end. The MILLENNIUM had arrived but no one realized its presence.

Now commenced an era of grand improvement in every way. Science, art, literature and mechanics were in the midst of the people. Everything benefited the many, nothing a chosen few. Disease disappeared as education advanced and the average age increased rapidly. Now I went among these great people in Liberia and Sunland, for they made progress nearly parallel to each other, and observed their social, mechanical and scientific improvements. The car of progress rolled smoothly on with liberty and justice to control its course.

Other nations progressed differently from the Sunland and Liberian people. A people of a country further south of Sunland on the coast and in one large valley of a river, who were called the people of Erolia or Erolians, never had any terrible revolution, but by slow and gradual steps acquired their liberty and kept in the march of progress.

They at first had a despotism which on demand of the people, without bloodshed was changed to a constitutional monarchy.

As the people grew in intelligence and greater love for liberty, one by one the prerogatives of royalty were given to the people or placed in the hands of their real representatives. Eventually the ywere their own political rulers, the king or queen having only social prestige and position. Then the salary of the royal occupants was gradually reduced to nothing and the offices became merely positions of honor; but the people thought they must have a king.

Royalty went begging, several refusing to abandon their private business, or distant heirs, suddenly called upon, declined to leave their native or adopted countries in other parts of the globe. After some time a humble farmer was found, as heir by default of two or three others; but he positively refused to serve. He had his crop of fruit to attend to, and the sensible community in which he lived could not dispense with his services. So the people of Erolia suddenly woke up to the fact that they had been practically without a king for a hundred years and hunted no more for royal princes.

The Erolians were a gray-eyed, tall, quiet people, very strong and fierce if hard pushed. They resembled in stature and general physical qualities the Liberians, being muscular, very large chested and highly intellectual.

But in the far south side of the ocean lived a haughty black-eyed, coarse-haired people, who ruled by their intelligence and cruelty, the cringing, very ignorant black negrettoes. These slaves were too cowardly to fight stubbornly for their rights and too treacherous to each other to combine. They never used the bombs to destroy their masters to any great extent and the foreigners who came to help them were generally received coldly or betrayed. Not until all the other nations had acquired liberty, peace and prosperity did these people obtain their rights. Then in the name of humanity the other nations demanded that this slavery should be stopped, the land made free and their trickery government abolished.

It was done; but it took years to teach the aristocrats that they were masters no longer.

CHAPTER IV.

Science is a child as yet,
But her power and scope shall grow,
And her secrets in the future
Shall diminish toil and woe;
Shall increase the bounds of pleasure
With an ever-widening ken,
And of woods and wildernesses
Make the homes of happy men.   MACKAY.

Through all these observations Psycho had remained with me pointing out many things as I came to them, and briefly explaining phenomena and occurrences that puzzled my understanding. These people developed in many ways different from ours. Steam was never extensively used as a motive power, but gas engines were used at first to propel boats. Locomotives on railroads were used to more bulky and heavy articles, but did not come into rapid transportation of people until sometime after electricity was introduced as a motor.

Until the revolutions were over the mechanical improvements stopped where they were when the wars broke out. But at the final triumph of the people, inventions and prosperity took rapid strides. We walk through the wide streets of Liberia and on every hand are evidences of liberty and happiness. Where were once the narrow roughly-paved streets and alleys of the lower portion of the city, now are broad smoothly laid avenues with shaded sidewalks, a row of handsome trees in the center and statues or drinking fountains at every corner. Brown, black, gray and white stone houses of large size and beautifully ornamented are on every side. In the busy portions of the city, where the ocean electric boats are at the busy wharves, or the broad-gauged electric engines are coming and going with their heavy loads, the city is still open and no crowding is permitted. The stores and business houses have open plots of ground all around them and are no more than two stories high.

The ground floors are handsome stores, or well filled store-rooms. In some are heard the hum of busy machinery; in others the laughter of children at their play.

Here is an immense building of heavy stone and very little ornament in the center of a large block. We learn that this is a national granary and the train of cars being backed out of doors has been unloading the tons of white grain brought from a valley away to the north on the other side of those dark, high mountains. We pass to a large, handsome building close to one of the main avenues, and go with the stream of ladies and children through its broad glass doors and find ourselves in an immense oval hall, lighted by large windows all around it. Many counters and tiers of shelves are piled high with delicate fabrics and beautiful cloths. The scores of busy girls, ladies and gentlemen waiting on the customers are not pale and waxen as we should expect to see, but rosy and healthy as if they did not toil and rush fourteen hours a day.

Nor do they; for long before the sun sets the windows are closed, the doors slid together and away go clerk and sales-woman in beautiful, swiftly-moving electric carriages that hold from one to forty, to their communities further out of town. Or they hasten to the various parks to race and exercise in various games, witness feats of agility or sleight of hand. Many go to the opened porticoed massive buildings and listen to the lectures, or perhaps swim in the public baths in certain parks or by the shores of the gulf. Six hours out of the thirty in their day is devoted to labor, the rest to recreation, education, enjoyment and sleep. No master can lock the doors of his factory and say, " Toil and starve, or starve any way."

Here the worker by the plying loom or the clanging anvil, the roadside or the bench, is not an employee but a part owner in all that his

community controls. Generally the communities where the individuals reside are the owners of the industries they engage in. But some are communities simply for convenience in domestic arrangements, and the individuals are part of a hundred different co-operative industries or concerns. Community life did not spring into existence until after the adoption of 'the last constitution, when conditions were favorable for their organization, and the people were waiting for something to save and utilize labor. So in less than a century of our time there were very few isolated households in either Liberia, Sunland or Erolia, the communities ranging from three families in the little mountain valleys to four hundred sometimes in the city of Liberia.

Communities of over three hundred families were found not to work as well as those of from one hundred up.

The usual time of marriage was from about eighteen to twenty-five years of our time ; and as a man did not require to be rich or to have a bank account, he courted and married when he was young, strong and hopeful. He and his bride took up their residence in the community of one or the other; and as poverty and intemperance never came in at the door of their home, love very rarely flew out of the window.

By proper education, attention to the laws of heredity and careful lives generally, mothers were not broken down with disease before their prime, and children were not brought into the world with sickly or diseased bodies or minds. For a woman to have over four children was unusual; to have none at all more so. For a child to die was rare, but the funerals of the aged were common.

The numeral system of all the people but one on this planet was a duodecimal one, represented by twelve signs, and twelve or any multiple being as easily written and calculated as we do ten or any of its multiples. Their year, called by them by a word meaning a circle, was equal to a very little less than thirty-one and a quarter of our years. This year they divided into twelve periods and each period into twelve months, these months being from sixty-three to sixty-five of their days in length. They calculated by periods as we do by years, and circles (revolutions of the planet around the sun) as we do by

centuries. Their watch dials were divided into twelve parts or hours; these into twelve minutes and these again into twelve seconds. The watch was a very narrow oval, the single hand or pointer moving across from end to end once a day. They were carried in a pocket of the shirt or coat, and were about three inches long and about half an inch wide, often highly ornamented. The clocks were similar but larger.

Electricity was in greater abundance in their world than in ours, and therefore more easily obtained. It was used as a motive power at every kind of work and art. The public buildings were lighted by its soft, regular and mellow light, and the private rooms and halls of the communities, in city and country, were lighted only by it. Electricity also propelled their boats, ran their machinery, drew their loads of grain or merchandise, cooked their food, heated houses, and furnished power to drive their swiftly-gliding, unequally-wheeled carriages, or to haul their smaller loads of fruit or produce to market.

Smooth highways of somewhat elastic but artificial stone ran for hundreds of miles in several directions, with many branches and subdivisions, by-roads and cross-roads. Over these roads electric carriages of three, five, seven or nine wheels, and so on to any size that was convenient, could proceed with passengers or produce, at any desired speed not exceeding twenty miles an hour.

The motive power for all their machines, lights, etc., was cheaply and easily obtained by the power of water and wind. From the time the water began to run in the mountain courses it was made to store its power in reservoirs, or to light houses and run machinery close by, or have its power carried to a distance. At the numerous falls of the great national acqueducts and of the rivers, metal cases of about two cubic feet were filled with electric power and placed in engines to run them, or on the cars to be conveyed wherever wanted. From the mountains to the sea the water was made to fill power boxes or reservoirs to use in various industries. Water passing through the houses ran wheels that filled the electric reservoirs for lighting, heating and cooking, as well as for machinery, A box of two cubic feet was sufficient to run a small carriage a hundred miles or more.

In going through the city we notice a great absence of noise. The great engines on the railroads come in, switch, couple and uncouple from cars with comparative silence. The hundreds of electric carriages running up and down the avenues, or the little open narrow passenger cars on rails, drawn by electric motors, glide along the streets and highways swiftly and noiselessly, except for a whistle attached to the carriages that increased in loudness with the speed.

The foot-passengers on the smooth sidewalks glide along in soft shoes, like spirits. Only in the shops of the machinists and in the foundries is the clang and clatter heard; but even here the noise is greatly reduced.

Almost in the heart of the city the enormous house cats sleep in peace on the posts of the gates or in the porticos of the communities, with the sunshine streaming on their sides. It used to be the custom for each citizen to shut up a mother-cat with her kittens in the hall of his house at night. If a stranger by any means got into the house the cats would make a desperate attack forthwith, and being almost as large as a common wildcat is with us, the fight was a hard one. When not engaged in defending their kittens, under the same circumstances they would only caterwaul and scamper to whatever member of the household they liked best and awaken them. But now they had as little to do as watch-dogs; the halls of the communities were open nearly all night, and so the cats slept in peace.

I asked Psycho where were the public buildings, the capitol, the department buildings, the residence of the president, etc., so we went to about the center of the city and saw them. There in the middle of a large block stood a massive gray stone building of the usual oval shape, three stories high, with an oval dome, supported on pillars, above it. On this dome was a large statue of a woman, the Spirit of Unity, and at night from her outstretched hand shone a very bright electric light. During the day she held out a large three-sided blue banner with a yellow circle around a white field, in which were a number of pink stars. This was the national banner, the number of stars corresponding to the number of districts in the nation.

In the capitol building were a great number of small offices, and on the second floor was the chamber of representatives. This was only used as such about three of their months in a period; but the rest of the time was not idle, being occupied for lectures, balls, public meetings and national conventions.

Across from the capitol building to the south was a plain brown stone building, of the usual oval shape, and perhaps a hundred feet long. On a flag-staff in front of the main entrance is waving the national banner as a sign that the building is open, and over a portion of the door is an inscription in silver letters, meaning executive department. From the small interior hall or court are doors leading to various rooms, and on one side is a broad stairway. Over the doors are other inscriptions, meaning office of the president, office of the secretary of state, secretary of the treasury, secretary of industry, secretary of public improvements, secretary of intelligence, the last including the postoffice national institution. Up stairs were the offices of the private secretaries, clerks and the executive library. Many of the clerks were women; quite often a woman was in the cabinet, and when she occupied the presidential chair there was no revolution.

Near by on the same side is the patent office, about the same size as the executive department. Psycho tells me that its small size is due to the rule that machines that are used extensively are simply photographed, the model being stored away or given to some institution. Patents of no use are also treated in the same way; and so only a few models are exposed for a period or two, when they are followed by others.

On the north side of the capitol is the treasury, where the national notes are made, the money stored and the accounts kept. On the east side is the national clearing-house, where the accounts between the communities and individuals are balanced every six of their months, the government charging but a trifling percentage for the service. This is the largest of the public buildings except the capitol itself, but is only two stories high. It is built of stone, but of course oval in shape, square or angular buildings of any kind, either public or private, being rare. On the west side are the museum and the observatory. The former is next in size to the

clearing-house, but the observatory is mainly a hall of astronomical records, the main observatory being fully fifty miles away on the mountains. Next to it stands the national public library, a small building, as most of the books are in the many halls, colleges and institutions of learning in the various cities of the republic and in the city of Liberia itself. On another block is the general postoffice and electric signal department, which occupies considerable space, but I do not go to it.

I am disappointed in seeing that this nation of thirty millions of prosperous people have such plain and small public buildings, all of them not equaling in expense the state buildings of the little State of Connecticut, in my own country on Earth. Psycho listens to my observations, and answering numerous questions patiently until we get through looking over the buildings, and then replies while we proceed to other points of interest:

"You are used, my son, to useless and expensive display of massive and empty public buildings. Here the people have learned that it is more than useless to put the wealth of the nation into piles of stone, only to be used a few days out of a period. The president is only the chief clerk of the people, and not having the arbitrary powers or dignities of a sovereign, as the president of your country on your planet, he is not called upon to display extravagance or to keep up the dignity of the state. Therefore no mansion or palace is furnished him for a residence, it being considered sufficient to appropriate an office for his business with a number of assistants. Vast armies of clerks are not needed to dispose of the people's wealth, and buildings are not erected to be used a few days out of a period. Every building erected by the people is in continued use, and the capitol is not used as a saloon or restaurant, nor has it but three committee-rooms around the hall of representatives. Any national convention can obtain the use of this hall in demanding the keys. The wealth of a nation is displayed not by the magnificence of its public buildings or the extravagance of its highest officials, but by the actual prosperity of its people and the equal distribution of the products of labor.

"Rear a mountain of granite over the body of a dead ruler, and you mix the mortar with the blood of slaves. Pile up national buildings costing millions of days of labor, and you build a sepulcher for liberty. Borrow of the future to commemorate the past, or to satisfy the arrogant assumptions of the present entrusted with the country's welfare, and you enslave unnumbered generations, plant the seeds of tyranny and corruption, bind liberty in chains, and destroy the prosperity of a nation. These people have learned that they can but show their strength and prosperity to others by prosperous communities, equal wealth and intelligent citizens."

Thus rebuked for my criticism of the manner of public building, Psycho continued:

"With the experience of centuries of oppression and debt, these people learned that it would be better for their representatives to meet on the open square, and the public buildings to be of the flimsiest and cheapest construction, than to bind burdens on the shoulders of their children, or to incur a debt of any kind. Therefore in letters of blood is written in their constitution: 'No private debt shall ever be considered binding or have any standing in law or justice, and no public debt shall ever be incurred for any object or under any circumstances.' Thus an immense amount of litigation, cumbersome legal machinery and untold expense were gotten rid of. Of this constitution I will tell you more by and by."

Printing was never used as we understand it. For many years they simply copied by hand, and although printing was afterward invented, it came too late to be of use.

Photography came before printing had got beyond rude wooden blocks, and it was soon used for obtaining cheap and accurate copies of works, then for newspapers, circulars, etc. By going into that branch of photography, inventions were brought out that enabled them to take thousands of photographs of a page of manuscript with a few hours labor; and thus books, pamphlets, papers, and everything we print, were photo-printed. Their books and manuscripts were generally of an oval shape, or perhaps the corners of a parallelogram simply rounded. The phonetic characters ran from left to right, but continued in the next page, not in the underside of the same page; and in

arriving at the end of the book was turned upside down, as well as over, thus bringing the conclusion on the same page as the commencement.

. Their knowledge of astronomy far exceeded ours, as by some means they combined photography with the telescope, so as to greatly increase the distinctness of the viewed object. They did not stop with simple photography, but were enabled to obtain photographs so clear that the picture looked almost like the reflection of a mirror.

After the era of liberty, the people drifted into a hopeful scientific materialism and abandoned the superstitions of their ancestors. The various nations of the world commingled until they spoke one common language and were one race. As by better social conditions they grew purer and attained a greater degree of sensitiveness the fact of immortality became better known, until eventually in every community those who had passed to a higher plane of existence were not lost to their friends, but met face to face, and the river of death was spanned by purity and love.

At my earnest solicitation Psycho enabled me to go into the public library of the nation and to look over their constitution, which was simple, short, and because of their intelligence and dislike of technical interpretations was easily, cheaply and effectively administered. In fact there was very little law; for the people did not need it. Their constitution was easily understood by them, their words conveying more than ours do; and the will of the people was first and highest above any branch of the government.

CHAPTER V.

" Balked are the courts and contest is no more.
Despairing quacks with curses fled the place,
And vile attorneys, now a useless race."   Pope.

Abstract of the Constitution of the Republic of Liberia (of the Planet Utopia.)

As it is necessary for the preservation of Liberty, the maintenance of Justice and the co-operation of the people in building public works, educating the citizens of the nation, that there should be a form of government, the Representatives of the people of the Republic of Liberia, form the following constitution:

Article 1. This provided for the rights of citizens, and that any person over ten " periods" of age who could read and write Estravlian, the national language, without regard to sex, race, religion, or residence (if native born), could vote and hold any office in the gift of the Republic. Foreign born citizens could hold any office after being residents and citizens a certain time.

Sections third and fourth provided jury trials, but for crimes of less magnitude than murder, the prisoner could have a jury of not less than three nor more than twelve. A majority, in minor offenses could find a verdict; in case of a tie, the judge having a casting vote; but in murder trials, the verdict was required to be unanimous.

Section fourth provided that the State could not take the life of a citizen for any crime; but on conviction of murder the second time or for money, at the option of the jury the prisoner could be branded in the forehead and transported to a deep valley from which escape was impossible.

Article second provided for the form of government. This consisted of three branches—legislative, executive and judicial. Sections first, second and third provided that there should be one representative to every thirty thousand citizens, to be elected once every period and to receive a salary of six thousand royars a period,

a royar being equal in purchasing power to about one dollar and a half.

The representatives could meet but once in a period, (two years and a half,) and could only continue in session three months and sixty-five days each, unless permitted to sit six days longer by the president. They could, however, be specially convened by a call of the people, or the president.

Secs. fourth and fifth provided that they could pass laws and make treaties, issue legal money, make appropriations, levy taxes, construct public works, provide for the education of the people, or anything that the people might entrust to them.

Sections seven and eight provided that a law passed by them could only be vetoed by the people; and a bill having passed the Representives could be put before the people, on a demand of one-fourth the representives or about one million and a half citizens. Any bill defeated by a majority of four or less could be put before the people on demand of a number equal to the minority or the same number of citizens; but any bill defeated by a greater majority could only be put before the people on the demand of a morjority of the representatives, or about three million citizens. Any decision of the judiciary could be considered by the representatives.

Sections nine, ten and eleven provided, for the executive, which consisted in executing the laws, carrying on public improvements or any other business that might be entrusted to them by the representatives or the people. There was no Vice President; but in case of the death, disability or resignation of the President, the presiding officer became President until the end of the term, or the convening of the representatives, when a president was elected by

them. Next to him were the members of the Representatives in order of their age.

The national judges were one to every six hundred thousand citizens, and were elected for a term of four periods.

But the judges at the end of the judiciary section were warned as follows: "Judges of the national courts are warned against making discussions on trifling and technical grounds or against considering cases of no importance to the Nation and interfering with the administration of justice by the lower courts.

Section third was on limitations of legislation. Liberty of speech, religion, of the press, of public assembling, of free travel, or of bearing arms in any way, could not be interfered with. No private debt could be made binding, but the laborer was to be considered as part owner of the property until his or her wages were paid. No public debt could ever be contracted under any circumstances; nor could the volume of the currency be increased or decreased over thirty royars per capita. No aid or countenance could be given to any religious institution, educational college or school, or any individual for any purpose, object or service, real or imaginary. Section nine provided that no law increasing the salary of any public officer, elected or appointed, could be passed without the consent of two-thirds of the people. No law could be passed that was over two hundred words long or that embraced more than one subject.

No law operating especially in one district or section of the country could be passed without the consent of that district or section.

Article four treated of public property, and section first declared that " land is the common property of the people, and with the water, or anything that the people may consider public, shall belong to the people." Citizens by cultivating a certain portion of the land might cultivate a certain small amount of land equal to about six acres. Communities could control land up to about one thousand acres, according to the number of persons in a community. No water or land could be leased or granted to any individual or corporation for service or construction for the government. Section five provided that all highways, rivers, means of transportation, or anything of national importance, should be in the hands of the people.

Article five treated of political divisions, by which the republic was divided into districts of as nearly as possible, one hundred and forty-four thousand citizens in each. Every district had a district judge and a council or legislature elected by the people. The districts were again divided into districts of as nearly as possible twelve thousand each, and had a justice who, in like manner, was elected by vote of the people. The people of a district had the veto power over the acts of the council or legislature or tie decisions of the district judge, the same as the people of the republic in national affairs.

Article six regulated methods of election, and provided that for any office where the number entitled to hold the office exceeded one, such as a district council, national judge, or national representative, the citizens were entitled to but one vote for one candidate; with an alternate. The alternate could only be valid when the first choice proved to have a surplus of votes over the number necessary to election or to lack the required number. The candidates who received the highest number of votes cast were to be declared elected to the number required.

When there was but one entitled to hold an office such as president, district judge, or division justice there was but one vote and no alternate; the candidate receiving the plurality of votes being elected.

When in a list of those candidates receiving the lowest number was duplicated the native born candidate was first in rank over one of foreign birth.

But if both were natives or both foreigners, the elder took precedence. This case however very rarely occurred.

It was especially declared that the people of the republic were to be the final appeal on any case, question, discussion, law, or whatever might be of national interest. And all officials were warned that they were the servants of the people, and that the nation could only keep its dignity by the prosperity of the people and the simplicity of its officers and servants.

The last section of the constitution read:

" This constitution may be amended, changed or overruled at any time by the people, and the passing of any law by the vote of the people

shall make it above any constitutional provision whatever. The people are to be the rulers of themselves."

Approved by the people by direct ballot by a majority of three millions of citizens (whole number of citizens about ten millions), on the 38th day of the fifth month, third period of the second circle of liberty.

Of course as time went on several important changes were made in the constitution, and when made were simply inserted in the articles and sections where they belonged. The voting was very simple, and the tickets rarely consisted of over a dozen candidates. An election of the nation generally took place at a different time from the election of the districts. The offices to be filled were photo-printed on oval ballots from three inches to one foot long and about three inches wide. The citizen voting had to write the names of the candidates under the printed titles, and any number of citizens could demand to see the ballots.

A citizen was not obliged to write in his or her hand-writing the names of the candidates desired, but could disguise their hands. On voting the citizen wrote his or her name opposite their name on the Register, and thus proved their eligibility as well as prevented any fraud. The election usually occupied two days; but the polls were open about six hours daily, and then only before and after working hours, that by strict enforcement of law could never exceed six hours out of their days and nights of thirty hours. It was considered a disgrace not to vote, and a citizen whose name was not written in the register during an election had to give some valid reason for the omission, as well as pay a fine. Any citizen who without such a reason did not vote a certain number of times in succession was deprived of citizenship, and was considered a foreigner, the citizenship only being acquired by a continued residence the same number of years as required for the foreigner to become a citizen. Any representative of the people, either on the judge's bench or in the national representatives, who did not vote on three bills, or was absent more than one day in a session, lost his or her seat, and the one standing next on the list of candidates at the last election took the place.

For a representative or other "servant of the people," as they were called, to thus lose their place meant political death as well as social disgrace. It was looked upon in the same light as we would regard an officer who resigned during a battle. When the representatives met, they went to work like so many industrious clerks, and for a member to speak over ten minutes, unless a very able and highly respected citizen, meant immediate voting down. Order was observed, and during the session the representatives made very little noise. If any member on any question spoke over half an hour, no matter how highly respected, some one would rise and notify the representative that there were plenty of steps, public parks and temples of science in the city of Liberia, where the people as well as the representatives would be pleased to listen after working hours.

At first when the constitution was adopted, it was necessary to keep a large force of police in the cities to defend citizens and to see that municipal laws were not overridden, and the justice's court was kept quite busy; but these conditions quickly died away as individuals were absorbed into communities. For a person to be attacked and robbed was of such unusual occurrence that often for years a justice would have no such case to try. Murder was very rare, but sometimes did occur under extreme aggravation. Arbitration between individuals and communities became the most common manner of settling differences when the efforts of friends could not obtain satisfaction to both parties. If arbitration was once decided on there could be no appeal to law, as it was considered better that a little injustice be suffered than that the courts should be overburdened with petty cases.

So the people gradually found themselves with closed courts, no police except night watchmen for fire, so little law that it was hardly heard of, but plenty of justice. The streets were lighted by electric lamps that cost comparatively little. The citizens voted at the elections or moved about in daily intercourse, with no jars or fights. The prisons were simply workshops and asylums, and about three hundred years after the adoption of their constitution a prison was almost unknown.

At first a murderer was put to work and paid

full wages for his services, being charged with his board. The savings were divided between the family of the murdered person, if they required it, for a certain time, and the prisoner. Other criminals were treated the same. After a given time more liberty was granted them; and if for many years a murderer acquitted himself of any criminal nature by industry and good behavior, he could be pardoned by a vote of the people in the district where he committed the crime. But for a second murder the criminal was branded in the forehead and sent to a valley, from which escape was impossible. They generally preferred to breathe a poisonous gas and die, however, rather than go to the valley, the option being usually accorded to them.

The population of Liberia never numbered more than thirty-five millions of people, and at the time of the adoption of the "last constitution," as it was called, the population numbered about twenty-five millions. For about three centuries they slowly increased to thirty millions, notwithstanding the changing conditions of the planet. For about a thousand years they held their number pretty well; but at last they began to slowly lose ground. Hardly perceiving it at first, they began to realize it after a while.

The representatives in meeting passed appropriation bills and one or two laws necessary to start some public work. This they did on the first and second day. On the third day, after waiting to see if anything further was to be done, they generally adjourned. To sit over a week of five working days was very unusual, and to hold a session six weeks was of as much importance to their history as war is to us.

The main business of the government was to construct aqueducts and keep up the highways and railroads. Water was the most difficult thing to obtain; but by the most skillful construction of aqueducts and reservoirs, and the running of tunnels into the very hearts of the mountains, a sufficient quantity was obtained to satisfy all requirements. District and national bodies of representatives concerned themselves with such matters alone. The people needed no laws, and what few questions did come up were decided without looking at the constitution or any book of law, justice alone weighing in her scales the issue.

In spite of the lowering ocean, the rising mountains, the valleys filling with precipices, the abandoned cities and the falling rivers, the people grew in intelligence, though standing almost still in mechanics. They fought Nature with heroic spirit, and looked her square in the face.

CHAPTER VI.

" The stars shall fade away, the sun himself
Grow dim with age, and nature sink in years;
But thou shalt flourish in immortal youth,
Unhurt amid the war of elements,
The wreck of matter and the crush of worlds."

ADDISON.

Early in the dawn of civilization the idea of a future life was entertained by many people. And even before, when man was a wild and naked savage, he worshiped the spirits of his ancestors and bowed to men immortalized in tradition as gods.

But the centuries failed to bring any more than a simple hope and belief to questioning man. The priests kept the people in ignorance, and only used this hope to enslave their followers.

In Liberia, after the establishment of the last constitution, the people drifted into a hopeful, calm and brave materialism. So disgusted were they by the acts of the priests in past ages that all forms of belief in immortality were classed with the dead superstitions of the past.

Early in the history of the nation as a republic, messengers from the other side of life had made themselves manifest to mortals in the flesh. Slowly but surely the glad tidings spread. In spite of mistakes and dissensions, of fraud and ignorance, the fact that man existed after death continued to be demonstrated. At first the various religious sects of the civilized nations bitterly opposed the idea, and not until they were about to fall to pieces before the growing enlightenment of the people did the priesthood espouse immortality as a fact and not merely as a vague hope or faith.

But the science of the day continued its attacks on the sophistry of these religions until there was nothing left of them to be united by but the fact of immortality. For fully a century spiritualism languished in the minds of the people of Liberia after the final downfal of aristocracy and priestcraft. Science, meanwhile, pushed on with rapid strides in material directions, but refused to consider the vital question: "If a man die, shall he live again ?" In all its branches science was growing, and the people under the stimulus of liberty were progressing higher, and higher, toward a more perfect civilization.

At length Spiritualism once more became a subject of investigation, and science with awakened interest turned her searching eyes upon its despised relation. The cool and quiet reason of the intelligent materialistic philosophers was slowly convinced, and one by one the Scientists of the nation openly advocated their convictions. Unimpeded by prejudice and credulity, its advocates were enabled to more successfully demonstrate and prove to the investigators this glorious philosophy. Carefully sounding and considering each successive step, and scientifically weighing each piece of evidence, the investigators became earnest advocates. By more harmonious conditions than existed when Spiritualism was opposed by the church, better manifestations were produced. The life of the people was such and the laws of Nature so followed that harmony was more prevalent. People were born better and were therefore better able to grasp truth, and to bring forth spiritualized children. Crime was cured at its fountain heads and, as a consequence, more and more people in each generation were able to receive immortality and not only receive but often to be the means of demonstrating it. When the faculties of mediumship, psychometry and clairvoyance became as common as the faculty of smelling once had been, people had to believe, had to acknowledge what was palpable to the senses.

Thus spirits were enabled to eventually make themselves tangible to the material senses and to clothe themselves temporarily with matter so as to be perceptible to all. Materialization at first in the dark finally was produced in the light,

but never got to a point where the form was actually the same as the form of the material body, never more than a shell or representation. The vital organs were not there, the blood did not pulsate, but simply as clairvoyance became more common the spirits became more real. The hand of the materialized spirit could be shaken, but as the friend held it the form faded into spirit and the grosser matter disappeared. On one occasion the friends met in a large temple or free college, and before several hundred invited friends, many of them scientific men and officials, a seance was given of great interest. Scores of spirits were rendered visible and several ancient leaders and statesmen appeared. One spoke for a few minutes from the rostrum which was exactly in the center of the building. After this several failures took place, because of endeavoring to carry on these seances before too strange and too large audiences.

But at last in the national chamber of representatives a seance was given where there appeared many spirits of both sexes who had passed away from earth as leaders in either science or liberty. The main medium was simply slightly concealed by a shawl or robe only as the spirit rose and formed. The spirit would advance and speak a few words first on one side of the central stage and then gradually passing around to the other side, as was the custom. One very venerable appearing spirit who had made many discoveries in science and who also had been an active defender of liberty, spoke for fully twenty minutes; then faded before the audience to a luminous cloud, reappeared for a moment, smiled and vanished.

More and more spiritualzed became the people until at every assembly the forms of the departed appeared and eventually mingled at pleasure with the crowd, exciting no remark. For as I stated, they could always be distinguished by the peculiar appearance of the matter composing the temporary mask and often disappeared to coarser eyes when in the vicinity of uncongenial mortals. The whole planet was new to the people and patriotism had extended to the entire globe, while humanity realized in word and deed that all were of one family; brothers and sisters.

As the centuries went on the population of the globe began to decrease in proportion as the amount of arable land contracted. The ocean grew smaller and deeper, the mountains higher and more barren, and as a natural consequence man was forced to follow the lowering waters. Science was brought in and prolonged the contest between man and inevitable law. Lakes were drained to furnish land, and the rocks that fell in avalanches into the deep valleys were conveyed away. By the application of electricity and various powerful explosives, long tunnels were driven into the hearts o the mountains for water and vast aqueducts conveyed it to public reservoirs. Highways, that often with the aqueducts ran through tunnels lighted by electricity, were constructed, and over these in swiftly moving electric carriages the people journeyed or conveyed the products of different localities.

By the failure of the water supply, the overwhelming of the land by avalanches and the increasing rarity of the atmosphere, communities decreased in number of inmates and valley after valley was finally abandoned by the last of its inhabitants after having been the home of their people for centuries. Not as many lives were lost by the falling rocks as we might suppose; for science was able to predict these events, and the people could remove out of danger.

But with the waning planet civilization did not recede; on the contrary for a considerable time it advanced. At last, however, it was forced to remain stationary, all the efforts of research and invention being devoted to its preservation, as Nature was now against progress.

Spiritualism, hand-in-hand with Science, became a universally acknowledged philosophy. with the heroic war on failing Nature the immortals were with the mortals giving words of advice, of comfort and of love. In the family and in the community they were ever present and recognized; took part in the joys and sorrows of their loved ones and continued to follow and to lead upward.

The atmosphere was always so rarified that flying as a means of locomotion was never attained; but from the tops of high mountains, by means of a machine with very broad wings and a body of gas, one or two persons for pleasure were enabled to fly *down* for a few miles.

By a gigantic series of labors the whole people of the planet tunneled through a range of mountains for several miles and drained a considerable portion of the waters of the ocean into the deep basin of an ancient sea, in order to make the low plains around it productive. In this they did not succeed so well as they anticipated; but still homes were made for several millions of people in this region. This drainage so lowered the East Gulf that after several years of wonderful labor its waters were drained and pumped out and a new valley created, walled from the main ocean by a mountain of masonry. But all these labors rendered the high plateaus to the north of Liberia only more barren and unproductive. As the new valleys were opened the high plateaus were abandoned, and the ancient valleys were left to black, tall precipices and barrenness.

After a few more generations the entire population of Liberia had congregated in the one valley of the gulf. The proud cities of the bygone centuries were left to crumble into dust, and over their ruins man could not go, for the vital air was so thin and water so scarce that it was impossible to exist in these cold and barren regions. But beautiful cities were below them, with happy, industrious and contented inhabitants, civilized and progressive as they had been for so many centuries. Science was made to war against fate, while poetry and song made harmony among the sons and daughters of the decaying world. Art and wit gave delight to the eye and mind, and with music was developed to a high degree of perfection. The voice was cultivated especially, and with the music was remarkably soft and expressive. Music conveyed ideas almost as definite as if there had been a language of melody. Vocal and instrumental music was cultivated in every family, and for a party of people to break out in joyous song was very common. A party of musicians would sing and play in one apartment, the sound being conveyed to the audience in another, and seeming to come softly from every part of the room. In their circles bevies of spirit children would often appear in spirit wreaths from the mediums to the ceiling and sing, while many mortals would join softly in the chorus.

As the population decreased, great difficulty was experienced in keeping up communication with the isolated and smaller valleys. When the public roads could no longer be kept open, tunnels were constructed, lighted by electricity, and driven through. But these often fell in, and then electric signals, through wires or as flashes in the air, were utilized to convey intelligence. Sometimes, when possible, hardy men would scale the mountains; but this, owing to the rarified air, could not always be done.

In one valley in the eastern portion of Liberia, great difficulty was experienced in keeping open the tunnel between them and the larger gulf valley. Once for several years communication was only had by electric signals until a new tunnel was constructed. But the affairs of the valley went on as before. Concerts, lectures, meetings and circles were held as usual; and despite the failing energies of the planet, the light of civilization continued to shine in brilliancy and power as nature drifted deathward.

Again, after enjoying full communication for a few years, the tunnel was crushed in, and the inhabitants isolated from the outer world. Rocks began to fall from the mountains, and fears were entertained of the complete destruction of the people if relief was not soon obtained. Accidents and natural decrease had reduced the inhabitants to about three hundred, when but a century and a half previously they numbered several thousand. Their countrymen worked from the outside and they from the inside; and at last after fifty years a small tunnel was completed. The remaining inhabitants fled, leaving their home to the crumbling rocks and silence.

This process of abandonment continued until every country was only represented by one or two valleys. The Gulf-valley of Liberia was one of the most productive and here many of the last of nations fled and were welcomed. More than one community, however, cut off from communication with their fellows, were forced to give up the fight and die amid the crash of falling mountains, isolated and alone.

One of the last places to fall in ruin was the valley of Sun-land where their lake had been. The people gradually gathered into this valley, and as the water became scarce they retreated all into one small valley and excavated dwell-

ings in the mountain sides where the rock was most durable. To dwell in caves was imperative because of avalanches; and by carefully selecting the most durable rock the cave-dwellings thus excavated lasted many generations.

These dwellings were nicely fitted up, for electricity warmed and lighted them. From the bark of the few and scrubby trees that grew in open spots or in the fertile little vales, with goat hair and feathers of domestic birds, cloths were woven into various fabrics. With soft dyes these cloths were dyed in harmonious colors; and man, though living in caves, once more, as at his origin, was civilized and happy. Glass houses were built covering many acres, the glass composing them being fully three feet thick, very elastic and transparent. Under its shelter vegetables were raised by the help of electricity. A smelting furnace furnished them with aluminum, and iron for mechanical uses was secured from the mountain veins. Electricity was obtained from the streams of water carefully stored for service. The land was carefully cultivated and all the resources of waning nature were used to increase the happiness of man and to keep the flame of civilization bright.

By the force of circumstances the people at last all gathered into one cave-community consisting of perhaps two hundred and fifty persons—all remaining of a nation once numbering millions. Here they lived for several years, only occasionally terrified by the avalanches of rock and debris falling into their valley.

One day the terrible roar of an approaching avalanche was heard as it thundered down the mountain side, carrying all before it. "To the caves! to the caves!" was the cry; and all outside hastened in and the flood of rocks and sand filled up high the fertile little valley. Several more followed and when the inhabitants reached the surface they stood on a mountain of rocky fragments.

The valley was utterly ruined, and it was only the matter of a few weeks when famine would stare them in the face, and the inevitable result would be death in misery and pain for all in the end. With courage they had faced the future, but now hope was gone and death was before them. Of death they had no fear, but from torture they shrank.

In their large and beautiful lecture-room the entire community assembled to consider their course, and with them their friends of another yet the same world were cheering their friends in their extremity with words of love and hope.

After carefully considering every possible means of escape, it was almost unanimously concluded that the only relief from lingering starvation was immediate death. A few could have lived in one little valley very difficult to reach; but it was only for a few years that even this was possible. So all voted for death and peace, although the attending spirits were loth to have it so. Still, as nothing else could be done they did not strenuously oppose it.

On the floor of the beautiful hall mats were spread and the chemists of the community in an adjoining room, from certain ingredients, manufactured a poisonous vapor. The beautiful chorus of melody came in from a group of singers in still another room; and as it died away it was caught up by angel voices bidding welcome to the mortals about to join them.

Side by side lay or sat husband and wife, father and son, mother and daughter, brother and sister, lover and lover, softly conversing or singing as the last moments approached. Fearlessly they had lived, and now as fearlessly they passed to a continued existence.

From the farther end of the hall came a blue vapor that hid in a curling fog the statuary and pictures on the walls. It enveloped the nearest persons in its mists, and inhaling its perfume they clasped, smiled, kissed, kissed and slept.

Slowly the vapor passed toward the end of the hall, and the last to close their eyes were two lovers that, with their arms clasped together, lay by a rippling stream in a recess of the wall.

Those who first slept arose as the last sank to rest and met the glad Angel of Deliverance, welcomed by the friends gone before, and turning to greet those crowding in their footsteps.

The electric lights shone on the forms so cold and beautiful until the supply gave out, save one, which kept vigil for many weeks; but it too ceased finally to burn; and the sepulcher of the last of a nation was in endless darkness as their immortal spirits were in endless light.

But this was not the very last of humanity on

this planet. By natural decrease and accident the remainder were gradually extinguished, and humanity was eventually only remaining in the valley of the gulf in Liberia. By gradual steps they were reduced to about seven thousand only at the time of the end of the Sunland people, of which they were informed by spirit friends. As the changes went on they were compelled to resort to cave dwellings, and in nearly every way to follow the same path as did the Sunland community.

But they did not shrink or mourn. Life was full of pleasure; love and joy were there in all their varied forms. Friends from the other shore came through the thin veil between mortal and immortal at pleasure, and toil and strife were unknown.

Wonderful were the labors of these people to preserve their existence on the failing planet. By means of electric machines and railroads vast masses of debris falling into the valley were crushed or removed, and thus soil for cultivation obtained. From the simplest fungi and lichens, mushrooms and various products, their chemists produced delicate and nutricious substances; and from the disintegrating rocks they obtained fertile elements for the sustenance of their crops and gardens. With science as a servant, they turned every possible thing to advantage, and lived in ease and even luxury. All shared alike and no one shirked or monopolized. Money was unknown and greed forgotten. Equality, liberty and justice reigned amid them all.

But in spite of their utmost endeavors they were reduced by accident and decay to a mere handful. They lived in one cave amid the chaotic ruins of what had once been a fertile and populous valley. Above them lay vast, bleak and silent plateaus that for centuries had been untrodden by man or beast. Down the sides of the mountains rushed the avalanche, or into the deep crevices fell the loosened masses of rocks. In the air flew no birds; in the tideless, stagnant sea, scarce a hundred miles across, swam no fish. On the vast desert where once had been the ocean, wandered no human soul or lived no creature. Of animals none remained on the planet save those protected by man. And in this last community they had but five or six goats, that fed upon mosses and shrubs

that by hard clambering they obtained upon the mountain sides. Then the planet, so devoid of life, made it more difficult for the immortals to communicate; and only by great efforts could they influence their friends sufficiently to have them realize their presence.

Even these managed to live and learn in pleasure, for they had science and studies, books, telescopes, and various instruments of science. Notwithstanding the appalling drawbacks to which they were subjected, they managed to make progress in some directions.

When the inhabitants were reduced to only four families, one girl refused to marry. Her cousin was too much like her in many ways, and she decided it was wrong to bring any more children into the world. He in a few years died of severe injuries received from a fall, and she soon followed. In a few years only one pair remained, and their child, with the aged grandfather. They had been obliged to construct a new cave, and because of lack of electric power and numbers, the cave was small and not very well finished. Before their parents died it had been decided to all die by clasping hands and receiving a shock of electricity; but at the last moment the wife refused. She refused even now to give up, and contended that it was their duty to live until the natural end.

One day when the young man was climbing over the mountains a terrific avalanche filled up the little valley and buried him far beneath a mountain of debris. The three remaining in the cave were unhurt, and leaving the baby the mother and the old man went to search for the husband. He had agreed with his wife, when living, that if he was accidentally killed at any time, he would come to her in spirit immediately. But so crushed, and so deep was the body in the fallen rocks that it was many hours before he was able to separate his spirit and find his way.

The old man was confident the husband was no more; but the wife was sure he would have come to her if he was dead, and frantically searched for him. The spirit friends, owing to the convulsion of the planet from the effects of some vast falling of mountains, were unable to clearly appear, and she would not listen to them anyway. The aged father searched till night and then, so changed was the appearance of the

valley that he lost his way. In groping along he passed near the edge of a crevice in the rock which treacherously gave way, precipitating him into the gulf below, killing him instantly. To his daughter he was soon able to appear and he told her all. Then, knowing beyond a doubt that her husband and her father were both dead, she returned in the morning to her forgotten and famishing child.

The high mountains now sent down vast avalanches, and for hours the terrible roar was all to be heard. The woman lay in a stupor, and in a few hours passed to the life of endlessness and left her nursing babe.

A calm succeeded the storm; and though the electric light had gone out, a diviner light shone in the little cave; for many spirits were awaiting the spirit of the last human being on the planet. The child soon rested in its mother's arms, and humanity no longer was bound to the dying world.

For ages the planet continued to exist after the departure of man. All signs of animal and vegetable life quickly followed humanity; and the ocean, from a sultry pool in a desert of sand, into chasms slowly sank, leaving only a mass of salt. Rain had long ceased to fall, even in the finest mist; and in due time the atmosphere disappeared, after the last drop of water sank in the hungry sands.

The planet was a vast, lifeless desert of black mountains, towering tens of miles high above sandy seas or gloomy valleys. Everywhere death and desolation reigned supreme; and at last even the great globe itself seemed to die. For the attraction of gravitation between its particles failed to keep them together, and the planet separating into innumerable fragments, whirled back by degrees to the parent sun as flaming comets and bursting meteors. Many in their headlong course came within the attraction of the earth; and where, as in more than one instance, huge meteors fell with fearful force, great changes took place in its physical conditions that modern Science as yet fails to adequately account for.

Again was I on my own earth and Psycho beside me was ready to depart. Gravely he answered my many and eager questions and received my thanks.

"Son of Earth," said he; "you have seen the life of a planet from infancy to dissolution. Rapidly have I shown to you the various stages of development and decline of life with the civilization of humanity. As a rule the larger a planet the slower but the higher its development. This planet we have seen was developed far in advance of your earth to-day; but before it had got well on toward perfection the energies of mind and material science were expended in keeping the lamp of civilization burning, and in securing the future of man. But with your earth the altitude of civilization that will be reached far transcends your comprehension or belief.

"Your descendants will have aerial navigation and go from point to point at a speed that now would be incredible. People of separate continents will then be neighbors, and the whole world be of one nation and of one language, because of the close relation which people will be brought into by means of science and education. Means of communication will be found between planet and planet, and many other things as incredible to your ears will come to be everyday occurrences. Methods of producing food will be discovered that will render only healthful and pleasant labor necessary. Government will only be an administration of public improvements, mental and physical. Man in relation to his fellows will be entirely controlled by his innate sense of justice; and as the brutes disappear, so will brutality die. The boundary between the world of matter and the world of spirit (which is but matter refined) will fade away. 'Spirits will walk as with mortals one,' and earth and heaven, so close together, will have no separating veil of ignorance and sin. And when your globe goes to feed the fires of the sun, humanity will still exist in countless globes around life-giving suns, learning and progressing. And those who have fought the battles of life on the planets will continue to learn of the wonders of Nature throughout the æons of a glad eternity. Son of Earth, for a time farewell!"

Psycho disappeared as mysteriously as he came; and I was left to ponder and to write.

"End there is none to universe of God
Lo! also there is no beginning."

Alfred Denton Cridge.

www.ingramcontent.com/pod-product-compliance
Lightning Source LLC
Chambersburg PA
CBHW021539270326
41930CB00008B/1308